MARY WILMER

DECORATIVE ART
OF THE
SOUTHWESTERN INDIANS

By
DOROTHY SMITH SIDES

With annotations by
CLARICE MARTIN SMITH

and a Foreword by
FREDERICK WEBB HODGE
Director, Southwest Museum

DOVER PUBLICATIONS, INC.
NEW YORK

Published in Canada by General Publishing Company, Ltd., 30 Lesmill Road, Don Mills, Toronto, Ontario.

Published in the United Kingdom by Constable and Company, Ltd., 10 Orange Street, London WC 2.

This Dover edition, first published in 1961, is an unabridged and corrected republication of the work originally published in portfolio format by the Fine Arts Press, Santa Ana, California, in 1936.

Decorative Art of the Southwestern Indians belongs to the Dover Pictorial Archive Series. Up to ten illustrations from this book may be reproduced on any one project or in any single publication free and without special permission. Wherever possible include a credit line indicating the title of this book, author and publisher. Please address the publisher for permission to make more extensive use of illustrations in this book than that authorized above.

The republication of this book in whole is prohibited.

Standard Book Number: 486-20139-2
Library of Congress Catalog Card Number: 62-353

Manufactured in the United States of America
Dover Publications, Inc.
180 Varick Street
New York, N.Y. 10014

FOREWORD

That there was keen appreciation of the art of decoration among the American Indians, and especially on the part of the women, one need only glance at the selection made by the artist-author of this book to be convinced. Indeed so rich in esthetic quality was, and still is, much of the art product of the Indians of the United States alone, that the artist-author has been compelled to confine her immediate attention to that of the Southwest, leaving to the future the extension of her studies, let it be hoped, to the decorative art of the Indians of other fields.

Mrs. Sides has made from a vast amount of material, especially in the Southwest Museum, as comprehensive a selection as possible of the designs on pottery, basketry, and other artifacts of the Southwestern tribes, and in this manner has presented a fair impression of what those Indians have accomplished in early and in later times. The copies were faithfully made, while the reproductions are such as no one can reasonably criticize.

The demand for such a work on primitive art as the present one has grown with the increasing interest in Indian art and beliefs. Schools have undertaken the study of these subjects in a serious way, and there never have been so many devotees of American ethnology as at the present time. We commend the present work as one worthy of an honored place in the growing library of aboriginal American art.

F. W. HODGE

Southwest Museum
Los Angeles, California

ACKNOWLEDGMENTS

Grateful acknowledgment is given to all those who have assisted me. Most especially my Mother, without whose help, both material and mental, there would have been no book. To Florence Daly and Helen Evans, reference librarians of the Riverside Public Library; Winifred W. Britton, former Librarian of the Southwest Museum; Charles Avery Amsden for his timely advice and encouragement, and particularly to Dr. Frederick Webb Hodge, whose kindness, help and well-deserved criticism is most deeply appreciated. Lastly to Thomas E. Williams of the Fine Arts Press, for his courage, perhaps rashness, in printing this book.

LIST OF PLATES

1. PUEBLO VIEJO, Arizona
   Geometric ornamentation of food bowls, exterior border repeats, interior circular motif.

2. FOUR MILE RUIN, Arizona
   Conventionalized bird patterns, circular patterns and border repeats.

3. FOUR MILE RUIN, Arizona
   Geometric motifs.

4. FOUR MILE RUIN, Arizona
   Naturalistic and conventionalized patterns, birds, clouds, and butterfly.

5. MIMBRES, New Mexico
   Geometric borders from exterior of bowls, interior circular motifs.

6. MIMBRES, New Mexico
   Naturalistic animal and fish, geometric circles and border patterns.

7. SIKYATKI, Arizona.
   Prehistoric animal and reptile motifs, butterfly and bird bodies.

8. SIKYATKI, Arizona
   Circular feather and bird patterns.

9. SIKYATKI, Arizona
   Development of geometric banding on exterior of bowl.

10. SIKYATKI, Arizona
    Geometric and naturalistic bird motif and border.

11. SHONGOPOVI, Arizona
    Bird and reptile motifs, exterior bowl decoration.

12. HOMOLOBI, Arizona
    Bird and insect motifs, geometric and symbolic border pattern.

13. TESUQUE, New Mexico
    Highly ornamented exterior plan of bowl decoration, naturalistic borders.

LIST OF PLATES

14. PECOS, New Mexico
    Bird and geometric patterns.

15. CHEVLON, Arizona
    Geometric exterior bands, interior bowl ornaments.

16. DEVELOPMENT OF BIRD SYMBOLS

17. TRIBAL BIRD FORMS
    San Ildefonso
    Zuñi
    Acoma
    Hopi

18. HOPI KACHINAS
    Sio Humis Kachina
    Hokyana Kachina
    Kau Kachina
    Sio Kachina

19. SIA, New Mexico
    Naturalistic and conventional border patterns.

20. SIA, New Mexico
    Circular representation exterior of bowl; leaf, flower, and geometric motifs.

21. SAN ILDEFONSO, New Mexico
    Ancient polychrome patterns

22. SAN ILDEFONSO, New Mexico
    Modern polychrome, black-on-black, red-on-red ware.

23. SAN ILDEFONSO, New Mexico
    Motifs from paintings, conventionalized border repeats.

24. ACOMA, New Mexico
    Ancient bird and butterfly circular motif, naturalistic animal border, geometric border.

25. ACOMA, New Mexico
    Circular repeats, conventionalized border patterns.

26. SANTO DOMINGO, New Mexico
    Exterior ornamentation of bowls.

27. SANTO DOMINGO, New Mexico
    Geometric and conventional circular pattern and borders.

28. ZUÑI, New Mexico
    Ornamental borders and motifs.

29. ZUÑI, New Mexico
    Bird forms and conventionalized borders.

30. ZUÑI, New Mexico
  Border repeats, bird forms, and helix.

31. LAGUNA, New Mexico
  Bird and flower repeated patterns.

32. LAGUNA, New Mexico
  Exterior border patterns.

33. COCHITI, New Mexico
  Ancient and modern motifs, circular patterns, and border repeats.

34. WALPI, Arizona
  Bird forms, naturalistic and geometric patterns, and repeats.

35. MODERN HOPI, Arizona
  Bird forms and symbols.

36. MODERN HOPI, Arizona
  Bird forms, repeated borders.

37. ZUÑI DANCE MASKS
  a Sáyatäsha
  b Hémishikwe
  c Úwanami
  d Yámuhakto
  e Shíwani

38. MARICOPA, Arizona
  Pottery, weaving, and basketry designs

39. MOHAVE, Arizona-California
  Bead work and pottery borders

40. SAN CARLOS, Arizona, and MESCALERO APACHE, New Mexico
  Circular basket designs.

41. WHITE MOUNTAIN, Arizona, and MESCALERO APACHE, New Mexico
  Circular basket designs and dress ornament.

42. PAPAGO, Arizona-Sonora
  Circular geometric patterns.

43. PAPAGO, Arizona-Sonora
  Circular designs, geometric bands.

44. PIMA, Arizona
  Circular basket, pottery, and shield designs.

45. PIMA, Arizona
  Geometric border patterns.

LIST OF PLATES

46. CHEMEHUEVI, Arizona-California
    Simple geometric borders.

47. NAVAHO, Arizona-New Mexico
    Modern rug designs.

48. NAVAHO, Arizona-New Mexico
    Figures of Gods and symbols from Dry Paintings of Dśilyidje-Qácal.

49. NAVAHO, Arizona-New Mexico
    Motifs from Dry Paintings of Dśilyidje-Qácal.

50. NAVAHO, Arizona-New Mexico
    Ancient and modern rug designs.

BIBLIOGRAPHY

ALEXANDER, Hartley Burr. Pueblo Indian Painting.
1932 C. Szwedzicki, Nice, France.

AMSDEN, Charles Avery. Black-on-White Ware.
1931 In Kidder, A. V., Pottery of Pecos, vol. I.
Yale University Press, New Haven.

1934 Navaho Weaving.
Fine Arts Press, Santa Ana, California.

BOAS, Franz. The Decorative Art of the Indians of the
1897 North Pacific Coast.
Bulletin of the American Museum of
Natural History, vol. IX, pp. 123-176,
New York.

BUNZEL, Ruth L. The Pueblo Potter.
1930 Columbia University Press, New York.

CHAPMAN, Kenneth M. Evolution of the Bird in Decorative Art.
1916 Art and Archaeology, vol. IV, no. 6, pp.
307-316, Washington.

1931 Indian Pottery.
Exposition of Indian Tribal Arts, New
York.

1933 Pueblo Indian Pottery, vol. I.
C. Szwedzicki, Nice, France.

COOLIDGE, Mary R. The Rain-makers.
1929 Houghton Mifflin Co., Boston and New
York.

CRANE, Leo. Indians of the Enchanted Desert.
1925 Little, Brown & Co., Boston.

1928 Desert Drums.
Little, Brown & Co., Boston.

BIBLIOGRAPHY

CURTIS, Edward S.
1907-1930

The North American Indian, 20 vols.
Cambridge and Norwood, Mass.

DIXON, Joseph K.
1904

The Vanishing Race.
Doubleday, Page & Co., New York.

DOUGLAS, F. H.
1933-1935

Leaflets of the Denver Art Museum, nos.
53-54, 69-70.

FEWKES, Jesse Walter.
1894

Dolls of the Tusayn Indians.
E. J. Brill, Leiden, Holland.

1897

Tusayan Katcinas.
Fifteenth Annual Report Bureau of Ethnology, pp. 245-313, Washington.

1901

Archaeological Expedition to Arizona in 1895.
Seventeenth Annual Report Bureau of American Ethnology, pt. 2, pp. 519-744.

1903

Hopi Katcinas.
Twenty-first Annual Report Bureau of American Ethnology, pp. 3-126, Washington.

1904

Two Summers' Work in Pueblo Ruins.
Twenty-second Annual Report Bureau of American Ethnology, pp. 3-195, Washington.

GODDARD, Pliny Earle.
1903-1904

Life and Culture of the Hupa.
University of California Publication in American Archaeology and Ethnology, vol. I, no. 1, Berkeley.

GUTHE, Carl E.
1925

Pueblo Pottery Making.
Yale University Press, New Haven.

HARRINGTON, Mark R.
1927

Form and Color in American Indian Pottery North of Mexico.
Reprinted from the Journal of American Ceramic Society, vol. X, no. 7, Columbus, Ohio.

HEWETT, Edgar Lee.
1930

Ancient Life in the American Southwest.
Bobbs-Merrill Co., Indianapolis.

BIBLIOGRAPHY

HODGE, Frederick Webb.
1923

Pottery of Hawikuh.
Indian Notes, Museum of the American Indian, Heye Foundation, vol. VII, no. 1, New York.

HOLLISTER, U. S.
1903

The Navaho and his Blanket.
Denver, Colorado.

HOLMES, William H.
1886

Pottery of the Ancient Pueblos.
Fourth Annual Report Bureau of Ethnology, pp. 257-360, Washington.

1888

A Study of the Textile Art in it's Relation to the Development of Form and Ornament.
Sixth Annual Report Bureau of Ethnology, pp. 189-252, Washington.

JAMES, George Wharton.
1901

Indian Basketry.
Privately printed for the author, Pasadena, California.

1914

Indian Blankets and their Makers.
A. C. McClurg & Co., Chicago.

1917

The Indian Secrets of Health.
Radical Life Press, Pasadena, California.

KIDDER, Alfred Vincent.
1931-1936

Pottery of Pecos, vols. I-II.
Yale University Press, New Haven.

KISSELL, Mary L.
1916

Basketry of the Papago and Pima.
Anthropological Papers of the American Museum of Natural History, vol. XVII. pp. 115-264, New York.

KROEBER, A. L.
1904

Types of Indian Culture in California.
University of California Publications in American Archaeology and Ethnology, vol. II, no. 3, pp. 81-103, Berkeley.

Basket Designs of the Indians of North east California.
University of California Publications in American Archaeology and Ethnology, vol. II, no. 4, pp. 105-167, Berkeley.

BIBLIOGRAPHY

LAUT, Agnes C.
1913
   Through our Unknown Southwest.
McBride, Nast & Co., New York.

LUMMIS, Charles F.
1893
   Spanish Pioneers.
A. C. McClurg & Co., Chicago.

MASON, Otis Tufton.
1894
   Woman's Share in Primitive Culture.
D. Appleton & Co., New York.

1904
   Aboriginal American Basketry: Studies in a Textile Art without Machinery.
Annual Report of the U. S. National Museum for 1902, pp. 171-548, Washington.

MATTHEWS, Washington.
1883
   Navaho Silversmiths.
Second Annual Report Bureau of Ethnology, pp. 167-178.

1884
   Navaho Weavers and their Work.
Third Annual Report Bureau of Ethnology, pp. 371-391.

1887
   The Mountain Chant.
Fifth Annual Report Bureau of Ethnology, pp. 379-467.

1891
   Navaho Dyestuffs.
Annual Report of the Smithsonian Institution, pp. 613-615.

MINDELEFF, Victor.
1891
   A Study of Pueblo Architecture; Tusayan and Cibola.
Eighth Annual Report Bureau of Ethnology, pp. 3-228.

NESBIT, Paul H.
1931
   The Ancient Mimbreños.
Logan Museum, Beloit College, Wisconsin.

PAYTIAMO, James.
1932
   Flaming Arrow's People.
Duffield & Green, New York.

REICHARD, Gladys A.
1928
   Social Life of the Navaho Indians.
Columbia University Press, New York.

BIBLIOGRAPHY

ROBERTS, Helen H.
1929

Basketry of the San Carlos Apache.
Anthropological Papers of the American Museum of Natural History, vol. XXXI, pt. 3, New York.

ROBINSON, William H.
1928

Under Turquoise Skies.
Macmillan Co., New York.

ROSEBERRY, T. A.
collection of
1915

Illustrated History of Baskets and Plates, made by California Indians and many other tribes.
Panama Pacific Exposition.

RUSSELL, Frank.
1908

The Pima Indians.
Twenty-sixth Annual Report Bureau of American Ethnology, pp. 3-389.

SEYMOUR, Flora W.
1929

The Story of the Red Man.
Longmans, Green & Co., New York.

SLOAN, John.
and
LA FARGE, Oliver.
1931

Introduction to American Indian Art.
Exposition of Indian Arts Inc.,
New York.

SPIER, Leslie.
1933

Yuman Tribes of the Gila River.
University of Chicago Press, Chicago.

STEVENSON, James.
1883

Illustrated Catalogue of the Collections Obtained from the Indians of New Mexico and Arizona in 1879.
Second Annual Report Bureau of Ethnology, pp. 407-422.

1891

Ceremonial of Hasjelti Dailjis.
Eighth Annual Report of Bureau of Ethnology, pp. 229-285.

STEVENSON, Matilda Coxe.
1904

The Zuñi Indians: their Mythology, Esoteric Fraternities, and Ceremonies.
Twenty-third Annual Report Bureau of American Ethnology, pp. 3-608.

WESTLAKE, Inez B.
1925

American Indian Designs, First Series.
H. C. Perleberg, New York.

BIBLIOGRAPHY

WHITE, Leslie A.   The Acoma Indians.
        1932   Forty-seventh Annual Report Bureau of
                           American Ethnology, pp. 17-192.

Annual Reports of the Smithsonian Institution for 1884, 1891, 1928.
Annual Reports of the Bureau of American Ethnology for 1880-1881,
1882-1883, 1883-1884, 1884-1885, 1887-1888, 1893-1894, 1896-1897, 1899-
1900, 1900-1901, 1901-1902, 1904-1905, 1929-1930.

DECORATIVE ART
OF THE
SOUTHWESTERN INDIANS

Plate 1

PUEBLO VIEJO, ARIZONA. ANCIENT PUEBLO GROUP
POTTERY DESIGNS

Reference:
Two Summers' Work in Pueblo Ruins.
Jesse Walter Fewkes,
Twenty-second Annual Report Bureau of American Ethnology, 1904, pp. 3-195.

a   Plate LXIX, No. 177536a
b   Plate LXVIII, No. 177521
c   Plate LXIX, No. 177558c

The ruins of Pueblo Viejo are in the valley of the Gila river, Graham County, Arizona.

The designs of Pueblo Viejo pottery consist almost entirely of rectangular figures; examples of picture-writing are not found, nor pictures of birds, showing that the ancient inhabitants had not carried decoration beyond the geometrical stage. Their pottery was divided into the following classes; undecorated rough ware, decorated rough ware, undecorated red ware, decorated black-on-white ware, and decorated gray ware. An unusual feature of the decoration is, that the margin of the design is white. The decoration is both on the interior and exterior of vessel, and consists of rectangular bands and series of terraced figures, a prominent characteristic of all ancient pottery from Arizona.

PLATE 1

a

b

c

Plate 2

FOUR MILE RUIN, ARIZONA. ANCIENT PUEBLO GROUP
POTTERY DESIGNS

Reference:

Two Summers' Work in Pueblo Ruins.
Jesse Walter Fewkes,
Twenty-second Annual Report Bureau of American Eth-
nology, 1904, pp. 3-195.

a   Plate XXVI, No. 177203
b   Plate LX, No. 177048a
c   Plate XLI, No. 177223a

Four Mile Ruin is situated about two miles from Taylor, Arizona, and is one of the largest ruins in the vicinity.

The pottery found here, characteristically the same as that from the Chevlon and Homolobi ruins, consists of a decorated, and a rough coiled ware, the former prevailing. There is also a great similarity in the coarse pottery from Four Mile Ruin and that of Pueblo Viejo. The picture-writing on this pottery is highly instructive; bird figures are particularly abundant, also representations of human beings, reptiles, and insects. The picture-writing of each pueblo has an individuality which seems to indicate that it was independently developed, that certain forms or patterns were adapted to special ideals. The cause of this divergence in the designs is no more comprehensible than the difference in the decoration of modern pottery from the various pueblos.

PLATE 2

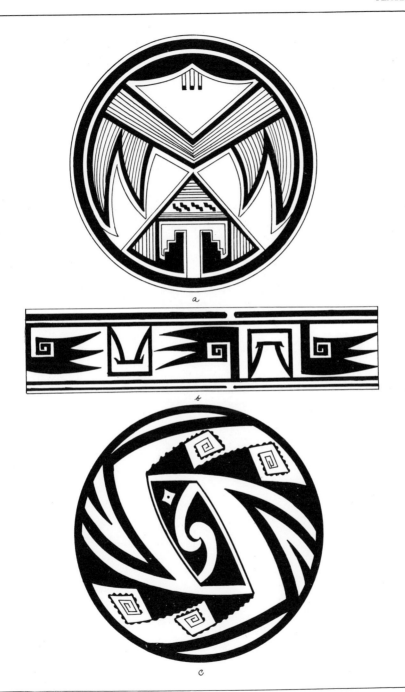

a

b

c

Plate 3

FOUR MILE RUIN, ARIZONA. ANCIENT PUEBLO GROUP
POTTERY DESIGNS

Reference:
Two Summers' Work in Pueblo Ruins.
Jesse Walter Fewkes,
Twenty-second Annual Report Bureau of American Eth-
nology, 1904, pp. 3-195.

a   Plate LXIII, No. 177162a
b   Plate XL, No. 177219a
c   Plate LIX, No. 177160b

Figures of birds predominate in the decoration of the pottery from many ancient
pueblos. In the delineation of bird figures the artists took strange liberty with nature.
In all representations of mythical animals the imagination had full sway. The por-
trayal was not that of a familiar bird, but a creature of fancy, distorted by mythological
conception or the whim of the artist.

Representations of feathers, often highly conventionalized, are freely used in
the designs on ancient pottery. One feather symbol is the triangle, a form of which
is still present in modern ceremonial paraphernalia. This type of feather design is
common, but is more difficult to recognize than that of the ancient Hopi.

PLATE 3

a

b

c

Plate 4

FOUR MILE RUIN, ARIZONA. ANCIENT PUEBLO GROUP
POTTERY DESIGNS

Reference:

Two Summers' Work in Pueblo Ruins.
Jesse Walter Fewkes,
Twenty-second Annual Report Bureau of American Eth-
nology, 1904, pp. 3-195.

a   Page 150, fig. 96, No. 177058
b   Plate XXV, No. 177293a
c   Page 157, fig. 105, No. 157352
d   Plate LXIII, No. 177147b
e   Plate XL, No. 177086b
f   Plate XXV, No. 177110b

The geometric decoration of pottery was common in all ancient pueblos. The
types were terraced figures, spirals, frets, bands, dotes, oblique and zigzag lines. The
proportion of geometric figures to that of animals was large.

The principal decoration was confined to the interior of bowls, but many are
found decorated with external banding. Figures of animals, unless highly conventionalized, and spirial designs, are rare, although straight lines and rectangular figures
were often employed.

Symbolic rain-cloud forms, combining the rectangle, semicircle, and the triangle, were freely used, the rectangle being the most common.

PLATE 4

Plate 5

Mimbres, New Mexico. Ancient Pueblo Group Pottery Designs

References:
Southwest Museum
The Ancient Mimbreños
Paul H. Nesbit
Ancient Life in the American Southwest
Edgar Lee Hewett

a
b
c Specimens from Southwest Museum
d
e

Ruins in the valley of the Rio Mimbres extend from an unknown distance below Deming to the headwaters of the stream in southeastern New Mexico.

The pottery is black-on-white ware and the standard form is the bowl, which is relatively deep and well finished. The decoration is usually confined to the interior of the bowl; the design is well executed, with a delicacy of line and an accuracy of spacing unequaled in other ancient pottery of the Southwest.

Aside from the extraordinary geometric designs, there is a profusion of naturalistic drawings, ranging from evidently mythical figures, to birds, animals, fishes, insects, and human beings.

True naturalism is so rare a phenomenon in all Southwestern pottery decoration, particularly in its early phases, marked by black-on-white wares, that its very high development is puzzling.

Certain bowls used as mortuary vessels, being placed over the head in burials, were always pierced in the base or "killed" to allow the egress of the spirit of the vessel to accompany the soul of the dead to its future world.

PLATE 5

Plate 6

MIMBRES, NEW MEXICO. ANCIENT PUEBLO GROUP
POTTERY DESIGNS

References:
  The Ancient Mimbreños
    Paul H. Nesbit
  Ancient Life in the American Southwest
    Edgar Lee Hewett
  Indian Pottery
    Kenneth M. Chapman

  a Page 352, Edgar Lee Hewett
  b Page 352, Edgar Lee Hewett
  c Page 352, Edgar Lee Hewett
  d Page 352, Edgar Lee Hewett
  e Page   9, Kenneth M. Chapman
  f Page 352, Edgar Lee Hewett

The ancient Mimbres people probably surpassed all other ancient Pueblo groups in their art, but they continued to live in pit houses, owing to the intense heat of the Mimbres valley. Although their living conditions remained the same, it was not so with their pottery.

All forms of corrugated ware, used principally for cooking, were familiar to them, and consisted mostly of food bowls with a gray background and black decoration; occasionally there is found black-on-white ware. Their geometric designs were not superior to those of potters of the western slope; however, their life forms were most striking, and in these motifs they were master artists.

These potters developed an esthetic imagination which produced an abundance of beautiful earthenware. The Mimbres valley is rightfully termed an "Ancient Art Province."

PLATE 6

Plate 7

SIKYATKI, ARIZONA. ANCIENT PUEBLO GROUP
HOPI PROVINCE
POTTERY DESIGNS

Reference:
Archeological Expedition to Arizona in 1895.
Jesse Walter Fewkes,
Seventeenth Annual Report Bureau of American Eth-
nology, 1901, pt. 2, pp. 519-744.

a   Plate CXXXII, e
b   Plate CXXXIV, a
c   Plate CXXXII, c
d   Plate CXXIII, c
e   Plate CXXIV, b
f   Plate CXXXV, b

The commonly accepted definition of Sikyatki, "yellow house," so far as the
general color of the pueblo is concerned, does not seem to be particularly appropriate;
but the name may refer to a cardinal point, a method of symbolic nomenclature fol-
lowed in the Southwest. The origin of Sikyatki is doubtful, however its builders and
occupants are supposed to have come into Hopiland from the valley of the Rio Grande
in late prehistoric times. It is almost impossible to estimate the population of this
pueblo at the time it flourished, but probably it did not exceed three hundred to five
hundred.

PLATE 7

a

b

c

d

e

f

Plate 8

SIKYATKI, ARIZONA. ANCIENT PUEBLO GROUP
HOPI PROVINCE
POTTERY DESIGNS

Reference:
Archeological Expedition to Arizona in 1895.
Jesse Walter Fewkes,
Seventeenth Annual Report Bureau of American Ethnology, 1901, pt. 2, pp. 519-744.

a   Plate CLII, d
b   Plate CLVII, a
c   Plate CLIII, b
d   Plate CXLVIII, d
e   Plate CXLVII, d
f   Plate CXLVII, e
g   Plate CL, a
h   Plate CXLVIII, c
i   Plate CLIV, b
j   Plate CLI, c

Sikyatki pottery is divided into three classes: (1) coiled and indented ware; (2) smooth, undecorated ware; (3) polished decorated ware. This pottery shows little or no duplication in decorative design, and every object bears different symbols. The decoration is chiefly on the interior of bowls, with geometric designs on the upper exterior. The first class, coiled ware, is coarse, not polished, and usually not decorated; the second class, undecorated ware, is as fine as that with painted designs; the third class, polished ware, of which there is the greatest amount, has more or less complicated designs and for this reason affords a more alluring subject for study than the other two classes.

PLATE 8

Plate 9

SIKYATKI, ARIZONA. ANCIENT PUEBLO GROUP
HOPI PROVINCE
POTTERY DESIGNS

Reference:
Archeological Expedition to Arizona in 1895.
Jesse Walter Fewkes,
Seventeenth Annual Report Bureau of American Eth-
nology, 1901, pt. 2, pp. 519-744.

a Page 708, fig. 286
b Page 709, fig. 289
c Page 709, fig. 290
d Page 709, fig. 292
e Page 713, fig. 306
f Page 721, fig. 329
g Page 723, fig. 337
h Page 726, fig. 347

In the decoration of Sikaytki ware mythical concepts are sometimes portrayed,
as the plumed snake. Reptiles, frogs, tadpoles, and insects are also fairly common.
Plants and leaves are seldom employed, but flowers are sometimes used. Probably the
most general motif found on the decorated pottery of Sikyatki is the feather, conventionalized, an important feature in the decoration of ancient Sikyatki and other Southwestern pottery. The employment of naturalistic ornament led to the use of rich and
varied colors, chiefly yellow, red, black, and white.

PLATE 9

a

b

c

d

e

f

g

h

Plate 10

Reference:
Archeological Expedition to Arizona in 1895.
Jesse Walter Fewkes,
Seventeenth Annual Report Bureau of American Ethnology, 1901, pt. 2, pp. 519-744.

a Page 722, fig. 335
b Page 683, fig. 272, plate CXXXVII, a
c Plate CXLIV, a

Birds and feathers far exceed all other motifs in the decoration of ancient Sikyatki pottery, the former being probably the first animal employed for that purpose. The food bowls thus decorated supply an abundance of material for scientific and esthetic study.

There is no reasonable doubt that figure 272, page 683, represents a bird, to which is attached a headdress of highly modified feather ornament. On each side of the body are undoubtedly wings, with feathers continued into arrowpoints. The tail is composed of three large feathers projecting beyond two triangular extensions, marking the end of the body.

On the upper surface of the vase are four similar designs representing birds of the four cardinal points. The wings consist of triangular extensions; each bird has four tail-feathers and rain-clouds on the anterior end of the body.

PLATE 10

a

b

c

Plate 11

Reference:
Two Summers' Work in Pueblo Ruins.
Jesse Walter Fewkes,
Twenty-second Annual Report Bureau of American Ethnology, 1904, pp. 3-195.

a   Page 117, fig. 73, No. 157771
b   Page 114, fig. 69, No. 157769
c   Page 114, fig. 68, No. 157817
d   Plate LI, No. 157784 a
e   Plate L, b
f   Page 117, fig. 72, No. 157134
g   Page 115, fig. 70, No. 157714

Comparatively little pottery has been excavated at the ancient site of the Hopi pueblo of Shongopovi, but the majority of that found consists of fine yellow ware smoothly polished and elaborately decorated. There is no essential difference in the forms of the pottery from this ruin and that from the pueblos on the Little Colorado. The picture-writing on Shongopovi ware closely resembles that on ware from ruins near the East Mesa of Hopiland. On the whole, old Shongopovi pictography is very similar to that of Sikyatki. Specimen b is an entirely different representation of the plumed snake, the feathers being represnted by two semicircular figures and the tongue by a line terminating in an arrowpoint. Many bird forms are present, with a close likeness to those of Sikyatki. A peculiar conventionalized form of "breath feather" here may lead one to regard this as a part of the mythical bird-man god.

PLATE 11

a

b

c

d

e

f

g

Plate 12

HOMOLOBI, ARIZONA. ANCIENT PUEBLO GROUP POTTERY DESIGNS

Reference:
Two Summers' Work in Pueblo Ruins
Jesse Walter Fewkes,
Twenty-second Annual Report Bureau of American Ethnology, 1904, pp. 3-195.

a   Plate XXII, No. 157588, a
b   Page 82, fig. 37, No. 156888
c   Plate XLIII, No. 156494, b
d   Page 76, fig. 31, No. 156603
e   Plate XXXIII, No. 156489, b
f   Plate XXXII, No. 156621, b

While four ruins are called Homolobi, ruin no. 1, situated three miles from Winslow, Arizona, is designated as the true Homolobi. It was a small pueblo of irregular shape, one exceptional feature of which is that the pottery was not buried with the dead as customary mortuary offerings.

Many beautiful examples of pottery have been found not far from the ruins of Homolobi, covered with pictographs which closely resemble those found in other parts of the pueblo area.

PLATE 12

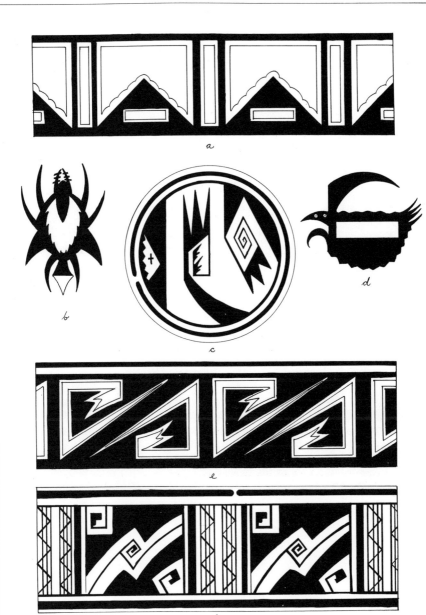

a

b

c

d

e

f

Plate 13

References:
Pueblo Indian Pottery, vol. 1, 1933.
Kenneth M. Chapman
Leaflets of the Denver Art Museum, 1933-1935,
Nos. 53-54, 69-700.
F. H. Douglas

a   No. 61, Leaflets of the Denver Art Museum
b   Plate 28, Chapman
c   No. 6, Plate 31, Chapman

The pottery of the present pueblo of Tesuque, New Mexico, was until recently quite distinctive from that of the other pueblos, the warm grayish slip being decorated in black only. The designs were complex, being built up of familiar symbols—the trefoil, meander, naturalistic leaf forms, and the plumed serpent which was typical of all Pueblo designs. These in combination form unique decorative elements.

Tesuque potters of the present generation have unfortunately given up the production of this traditional ware and now either imitate the products of other Pueblos or produce quantities of small earthenware articles gaudily decorated with aniline colors and designed solely for sale to white tourists.

PLATE 13

a

b

c

Plate 14

PECOS, NEW MEXICO. PUEBLO GROUP
POTTERY DESIGNS

References:
Pottery of Pecos, vols. I-II, 1931-1936.
Alfred Vincent Kidder
Black-on-White Ware
Charles Avery Amsden
In A. V. Kidder, Pottery of Pecos, vol. I, 1931.

a   Page 69, fig. 18, a
b   Page 79, fig. 24, f
c   Page 69, fig. 18, b
d   Page 65, fig. 16, d
e   Page 149, fig. 90, k
f   Page 115, fig. 68, b
g   Page 69, fig. 18, d
h   Page 87, fig. 34, h
i   Page 69, fig. 18, h

The pueblo of Pecos, abandoned in 1838, was known to have been inhabited as early as 1200 A. D. The pueblo became one of the largest and most important in the Southwest.

The Pecos women were excellent potters, and as their mode of living required pottery for cooking and serving food, as well as for carrying and storing water, a variety of receptacles were manufactured.

A profusion of black-on-white ware will be found, also a biscuit type consisting of a light tan or brown background with a black design. The interior of the bowls was the favorite area for the Pecos decorator; the design was usually in bands which began a little below the rim and extended to the line forming the bottom. Gradually the style changed and many new designs were introduced.

PLATE 14

a

b

c

d

e

f

g

h

i

Plate 15

CHEVLON, ARIZONA. ANCIENT PUEBLO GROUP
(SHAKWABAIYKI)
POTTERY DESIGNS

Reference:
Two Summers' Work in Pueblo Ruins
Jesse Walter Fewkes,
Twenty-second Annual Report Bureau of American Eth-
nology, 1904, pp. 3-195.

a   Plate XXXVIII, a No. 157119
b   Page 78, fig. 33, No. 157264
c   Page 83, fig. 38, No. 156138
d   Page 79, fig. 34, No. 157084
e   Plate XXXV, a No. 157406
f   Plate XXXVIII b No. 157184

The Chevlon ruin called Shakwabaiyki by the Hopi, or Blue Running Water Pueblo, is near Winslow, Arizona. The country at this point is sandy and almost barren of vegetation.

The pottery from Chevlon is distinctive, and excellent in craftmanship, with a general likeness to that from other Arizona localities. It is more varied in character than that from the true Hopi ruins, though in decoration there is much resemblance. While in the ruins of Chevlon there were many glazed bowls, pots, and jars, at Sikyatki no glazed pottery was found.

PLATE 15

a

b

c

d

e

f

Plate 16

DEVELOPMENT OF BIRD SYMBOLS
POTTERY DESIGNS

Reference:
Evolution of the Bird in Decorative Art.
Kenneth M. Chapman,
Art and Archaeology, vol. IV, No. 6, 1916, pp. 307-316.

a	Page 311	j	Page 312
b	Page 311,	k	Page 312
c	Page 311	l	Page 312
d	Page 311	m	Page 312
e	Page 311	n	Page 313
f	Page 311	o	Page 312
g	Page 311	p	Page 313
h	Page 311	q	Page 313
i	Page 311	r	Page 310

Of all forms employed as decorative motifs in primitive art, the bird has had the most widespread use. It has been a most adequate symbol in all aboriginal American art and particularly in the Pueblo area. The restricted use of conventionalized life forms is felt in the decoration of pottery, in which many motifs are taken from textile or basketry designs and retain their angular character though continually repeated.

Two types of pottery have furnished a profusion of material for the study of bird motifs, the biscuit ware and glazed ware from Pajarito Plateau of New Mexico. The greatest variety of treatment is found in the symbols from the glazed ware, and a large collection of these figures shows an unusual change from the realistic to forms which bear no resemblance to birds.

PLATE 16

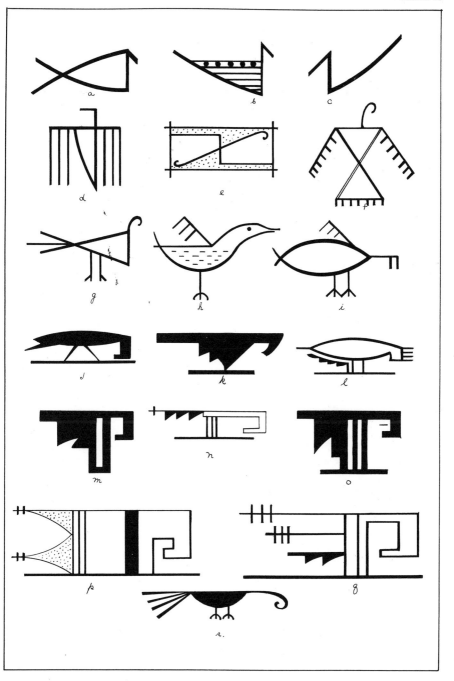

Plate 17

TRIBAL BIRD FORMS
POTTERY DESIGNS

Reference:
Evolution of the Bird in Decorative Art.
Kenneth M. Chapman,
Art and Archaeology, vol. IV, No. 6, 1916, pp. 307-316.

a   Page 316, San Ildefonso
b   Page 316, San Ildefonso
c   Page 316, Zuñi
d   Page 315, Zuñi
e   Page 315, Zuñi
f   Page 316, Acoma
g   Page 316, Acoma
h   Page 316, Hopi
i   Page 316, Hopi

In bird designs the rectangular form of a crooked head is the dominant characteristic. The greatest divergence is found in that part of each figure corresponding with the tail in the more realistic bird; this comes under the division of serrate, stepped, triangular, or linear, and is sometimes double or multiple in form.

The production of pottery is still an important industry in most of the Pueblos of New Mexico and Arizona. The designs of Cochiti and Santo Domingo, neighboring pueblos, show great similarity, though even here some small distinction is easily discovered.

PLATE 17

Plate 18

HOPI KACHINAS

References:
Hopi Katcinas.
Jesse Walter Fewkes,
Twenty-first Annual Report Bureau of American Eth-
nology, 1903, pp. 13-126.
Tusayan Katcinas,
Jesse Walter Fewkes,
Fifteenth Annual Report Bureau of Ethnology, 1897,
pp. 39-48.
Dolls of the Tusayan Indians
Jesse Walter Fewkes

a   Sio Humis Kachina, Southwest Museum
b   Plate XXXIII, Hokyana Kachina, 21st Report
c   Plate XXXIX, Kau Kachina, 21st Report
d   Sio Kachina, Southwest Museum

The Hopi Indians represent their gods in several ways, one of which is by per-
sonations, which are supposed to have magic power, capable of action for good or
evil.

Various symbols have been adopted to represent this power, and are portrayed
by "Kachinas" which are objects carved from wood or modeled in clay. The greatest
care is given to the representation of the head, and its size is generally out of proportion
to the other parts. It is painted in gay colors with various symbols.

Each clan, it seems, as it joined the Hopi population, brought its own gods represented by their kachinas. These were given to their children who were taught the
tribal legends, the heroic deeds of their ancestors, and the virtues of truth, honesty, and
chastity, by the medicine-men or the old women. Each doll has a name and different
characteristic markings; the representation of clouds, in some form, is very general,
and is supposed to have a spiritual significance, regarding water as the symbol of the
spirit, and prayer for rain—a prayer for that spiritual strength which comes only
through opening the heart to God.

PLATE 18

a

b

c

d

Plate 19

References:
Leaflets of the Denver Art Museum, 1933-1935,
Nos. 53-54, 69-70.
F. H. Douglas
Pueblo Pottery Making
Carl E. Guthe
Southwest Museum

a No. 64, F. H. Douglas
b No. 66, F. H. Douglas
c Plate III c, Carl E. Guthe
d Southwest Museum

Velino Shigi is an example of an Indian artist who has become very well known; he finished the fifth grade in the Government school at Santa Fe, when, untaught in the art of drawing or color, he was allowed to go on in the native method, in which no one can teach the Indian, and as a consequence one finds many beautiful examples of his art. With the Indian there is never any experiment with color or design, as the picture is mentally completed and then executed with precision.

PLATE 19

a

b

c

d

Plate 20

SIA, NEW MEXICO. PUEBLO GROUP
POTTERY DESIGNS

References:
Southwest Museum.
Dorothy Smith Sides, collection of.

a Flower motif, Dorothy Smith Sides
b Circular design, Dorothy Smith Sides
c Flower motif, Dorothy Smith Sides
d Circular design, Southwest Museum

The pueblo of Sia is on the Jemez river, 16 miles from Bernalillo, New Mexico. Originally its population was very large; it has decreased, however, until at the present it is one of the poorest, with only 150 inhabitants. The Sia women make an excellent pottery which closely resembles the representative type of Acoma. The colors used are red and black on a cream slip and is very often decorated with plant and animal forms, especially birds.

The particular combination and arrangement which is found at Acoma occurs again and again at Sia. In fact, so similar are they that often it would be impossible to tell from the decoration alone whether a jar came from Acoma or Sia. However, the clay of Sia is coarse and heavy, while that of Acoma is extraordinarily light and fine.

PLATE 20

a

b

c

d

Plate 21

SAN ILDEFONSO, NEW MEXICO. PUEBLO GROUP
ANCIENT POLYCHROME PATTERNS

References:
Southwest Museum
Pueblo Pottery Making
Carl E. Guthe
The Rain-makers
Mary R. Coolidge
The Pueblo Potter
Ruth Bunzel
Pueblo Indian Painting
Hartley Burr Alexander
Pueblo Indian Pottery, vol. 1, 1933
Kenneth M. Chapman

a Plate 25, No. 7, Chapman
b Plate 25, No. 14, Chapman
c Plate 35,   Guthe
d Plate 4, No. b, Guthe

San Ildefonso, an exceptionally interesting village of only about 100 inhabitants, is situated on the Rio Grande, not far from Santa Fe. The earthenware is of fine quality and exquisitely modeled, the beauty of a vessel depending upon the perfection of finish; ornament is merely to show by contrast the loveliness of the deep lustrous polish. The colors used in decorating the pottery are minerals, mostly ochres, with the exception of black, which comes from the guaco or Rocky Mountain bee plant.

With these people pottery is an important and profitable industry which has grown so steadily that its production has brought prosperity to the pueblo.

PLATE 21

a

b

c

d

Plate 22

SAN ILDEFONSO, NEW MEXICO. PUEBLO GROUP
MODERN POLYCHROME, BLACK ON BLACK, RED ON RED WARE

References:
Southwest Museum
Pueblo Pottery Making
Carl E. Guthe
The Rain-makers
Mary R. Coolidge
The Pueblo Potter
Ruth Bunzel
Pueblo Indian Painting
Hartley Burr Alexander
Pueblo Indian Pottery, vol. 1, 1933
Kenneth M. Chapman
Introduction to American Indian Art, 1931
John Sloan and Oliver La Farge

a   Southwest Museum
b   Southwest Museum
c   Southwest Museum
d   Plate XVII, John Stone and Oliver La Farge

The outstanding feature of San Ildefonso design is its restraint and brevity of expression; line is very important, and, too, the potters expend infinite time and pains in the process of polishing. They have developed a great variety of forms and decorations; their ware consits of a polished red, black-and-red on a light slip, and a polished black with designs in dull black. On all bowls the decoration is executed within bands which show considerable variety based on a small number of motifs. The most frequent decoration is the repetition of a single unit. The perfection of each piece depends on the precision of the maker.

PLATE 22

a

b

c

d

Plate 23

SAN ILDEFONSO, NEW MEXICO. PUEBLO GROUP
MOTIFS FROM PAINTINGS, AND CONVENTIONALIZED BORDER REPEATS

References:
  Southwest Museum
  Pueblo Pottery Making
    Carl E. Guthe
  The Rain-makers
    Mary R. Coolidge
  The Pueblo Potter
    Ruth Bunzel
  Collection of Mrs. Kenneth Worthen
  Pueblo Indian Pottery, vol. 1, 1933
    Kenneth M. Chapman

a   Mrs. Kenneth Worthen, collection of
b   Mrs. Kenneth Worthen, collection of
c   Page 125, No. 17, appendix 3, plate XXXVI, Ruth Bunzel
d   Page 125, No. 23, appendix 3, plate XXXVI, Ruth Bunzel
e   Page 126, No. 28, appendix 3, plateXXXVIII, Ruth Bunzel

Although polished black ware has been typical of San Ildefonso pottery since early times, it was not until Maria Martínez and her husband Julian, discovered, in 1921, the method of applying designs in self color, that this type of modern ceramics came into existence. She fashions her jars and bowls with such art that she has lifted her product into a class by itself. Her pieces are always graceful in form, admirable in design, thin and well fired, and altogether stamped with a brilliance of artistry that commands one's highest admiration. The painting is done usually by Julian.

PLATE 23

a

b

c

d

e

Plate 24

ACOMA, NEW MEXICO. PUEBLO GROUP
POTTERY DESIGNS

References:
Illustrated Catalogue of the Collections Obtained from
the Indians of New Mexico and Arizona in 1879.
James Stevenson,
Second Annual Report Bureau of Ethnology, 1883, pp.
307-465.
Introduction to American Indian Art
John Sloan and Oliver La Farge

a   Fig. 618, No. 39581, James Stevenson
b   Plate XVI, Ancient Acoma, John Sloan and Oliver
LaFarge
c   Fig. 619, No. 41316, James Stevenson

In western central New Mexico is the Pueblo of Acoma, "The City of the Sky,"
built 7000 feet above sea-level on a rocky mesa seventy acres in area with perpendicular
walls fifty-seven feet high. The pueblo is reached by precipitous clefts, up which all
material was carried to build the village. It is inhabited to-day and may be reached by
these same paths

Acoma was first visited by Spaniards in the year 1540. The story of the wars
fought on this mighty rock is so thrilling as to hold one spellbound.

Of all Indians, none are more resentful of intrusion than the people of Acoma, who
are unwilling to impart any real knowledge of themselves.

PLATE 24

a

b

c

Plate 25

ACOMA, NEW MEXICO. PUEBLO GROUP
POTTERY DESIGNS

References:
Illustrated Catalogue of the Collection Obtained from
the Indians of New Mexico and Arizona in 1879.
James Stevenson,
Second Annual Report Bureau of Ethnology, 1883, pp.
307-465.
Southwest Museum

a   Fig. 621, No. 41318, James Stevenson
b   Southwest Museum
c   Fig. 622, No. 42377, James Stevenson

In the pottery of Acoma one will find designs of trees, leaves, birds, and flowers, combined with geometric patterns; the colors used are black, red, and a creamy gray. The ware of Acoma is highly prized for its thinness and lightness, as well as for the wide range of its charming decoration.

The first delicate hair line around the top of a jar is never quite closed, the opening or space thus left is the "exit trail of life" through which the soul of the vessel may make its exit, for to the Indians every object is animate.

In addition to jars made for domestic use, there are vessels set aside for ceremonials. Sometimes funerary vessels were made solely for depositing with the dead.

PLATE 25

a

b

c

Plate 26

SANTO DOMINGO, NEW MEXICO. PUEBLO GROUP
POTTERY DESIGNS

References:
Southwest Museum
Pueblo Indian Pottery, vol. 1, 1933.
Kenneth M. Chapman

a   Southwest Museum
b   Southwest Museum
c   Southwest Museum

The pueblo of Santo Domingo is on the east bank of the Rio Grande in north
central New Mexico. It is the most conservative of the pueblos, and the people are very
jealous of white interference in their affairs. Pottery is still made by the women, who
form a heavy white ware with bold designs in black. The use of religious symbols for
decoration is forbidden, and the breaking of this rule would be severely punished.
Their vessels include large and small bowls, ollas, and huge storage jars, which serve
occasionally as drums.

PLATE 26

a

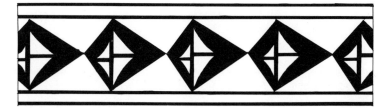

b

c

Plate 27

SANTO DOMINGO, NEW MEXICO. PUEBLO GROUP
POTTERY DESIGNS

References:
Southwest Museum
Pueblo Indian Pottery, vol. 1, 1933.
Kenneth M. Chapman

a   Southwest Museum
b   Southwest Museum
c   Southwest Museum
d   Southwest Museum

Santa Domingo slip, when applied, does not need to be polished with a stone, as is necessary with much of the Pueblo pottery.

The decorative art of Santo Domingo had been held to a severely geometrical system until the beginning of the present century, when the use of red, and the elaboration of plant motifs, led to the notable enrichment of the ancient art. The sacred combination of cloud, lightning, and rain symbols is still tabu, and these, if used singly, are hidden in formal arrangements of geometric and other units.

The "path of the spirit" or "exit trail of life" is often bounded by parallel lines extending vertically from rim to base.

PLATE 27

a

b

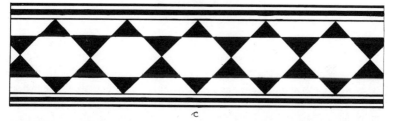

c

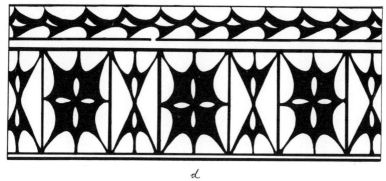

d

Plate 28

Zuñi, New Mexico. Pueblo Group
Pottery Designs

References:
Illustrated Catalogue of the Collection Obtained from
the Indians of New Mexico and Arizona in 1879.
James Stevenson,
Second Annual Report Bureau of Ethnology, 1883, pp.
307-465.

a Fig. 367, No. 40317
b Fig. 362, No. 41150
c Fig. 363, No. 41158
d Fig. 360, No. 39916

The Zuñi, who once occupied six pueblos, which through misunderstanding
were called the "Seven Cities of Cibola," now live in a single permanent village and
three summer pueblos on the Zuñi River in western New Mexico. They are a highly
developed people, both physically and mentally. From early times they were not only
skilled architects, but accomplished potters, weavers, and farmers, raising their crops
both by dry-farming and by irrigation.

Their ceremonies, elaborate and numerous, are often performed by masked personages who wear highly colored costumes replete with symbolism.

PLATE 28

a

b

c

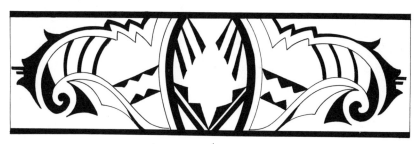

d

Plate 29

Zuñi, New Mexico. Pueblo Group
Pottery Designs

References:
Illustrated Catalogue of the Collection Obtained from
the Indians of New Mexico and Arizona in 1879.
James Stevenson,
Second Annual Report Bureau of Ethnology, 1883, pp.
307-465.

a   Fig. 427, No. 40290
b   Fig. 361, No. 39934, bird form
c   Fig. 428, No. 39954, leaf and butterfly ornament
d   Fig. 363, No. 41158, bird form
e   Fig. 361, No. 39934, Helix freely used
f   Fig. 363, No. 41158

Zuñi designs are conspicuous for their simplicity, balance, rhythm, abstraction, surpassing range of elements, and virility. These designs, which are of a type that has a recognized value of its own; consist chiefly of triangular figures, open circles, diamonds, scrolls, and arches. The pottery designs are usually divided into zones, and there is a rare combination of patterns; one never finds a meander or Greek fret, and there is a complete absence of vines and floral devices, except that on many of the water jars appear a conventionalized sunflower.

The colors employed in Zuñi pottery ornamentation are cream for the background, with black, red, and brown for the patterns.

PLATE 29

Plate 30

Zuñi, New Mexico. Pueblo Group
Pottery Designs

References:
Illustrated Catalogue of the Collection Obtained from
the Indians of New Mexico and Arizona in 1879.
James Stevenson,
Second Annual Report Bureau of Ethnology, 1883, pp.
307-465.

a Fig. 361, No. 39934, decoration belongs to third variety of design.
b Fig. 401, No. 40486, outside bowl design
c Fig. 362, No. 41150, bird form
d Fig. 360, No. 39916, Helix
e Fig. 365, No. 40312, bird form
f Fig. 365, No. 40312
g Fig. 362, No. 41150

Notwithstanding the oppression of the Spaniards in early times, the culture and
esthetic ability of the Zuñis flourished unabated, and they are still producing excellent
examples of their craft.

The colors of the Zuñis have a distinct significance. North is designated as
yellow, because the light of morning and evening in winter is yellow; West is blue,
for westward is the Pacific Ocean; South is red, it being the region of summer, and
the East is designated as white, to signify dawn. The upper region is multicolored,
as the light of the sun on clouds; the nether region, black, as deep caverns and
springs.

PLATE 30

Plate 31

LAGUNA, NEW MEXICO. PUEBLO GROUP
POTTERY DESIGNS

References:
Illustrated Catalogue of the Collection Obtained from
the Indians of New Mexico and Arizona in 1879.
James Stevenson,
Second Annual Report Bureau of Ethnology, 1883, pp.
307-465.

a   Fig. 585, No. 41295, broad oblique stripes and a figure
resembling blades of corn.
b   Fig. 616, No. 41297, little similarity to any other decoration it contains a scroll and abstract figures.
c   Fig. 588, No. 42386,large flower ornaments surround-
ing birds with a crest, and serrated figures.   One bird
represents a raven, the other a California quail.
d   Fig. 587, No. 42381, leaves designed to represent corn
blades, partially symbolical.

Laguna, the largest of all the Pueblo settlements east of the Continental Divide,
is situated on the south bank of the San José river, forty-five miles west of Albuquerque,
New Mexico. It is made up of a central pueblo, with a number of smaller ones. The
Lagunas are of exceptional intellect and physical development.

The Laguna dwellings are chiefly two-story adobe structures, architecturally
superior in point of construction to those of many Pueblos.

PLATE 31

a

b

c

d

Plate 32

LAGUNA, NEW MEXICO. PUEBLO GROUP
POTTERY DESIGNS

References:
Illustrated Catalogue of the Collection Obtained from the Indians of New Mexico and Arizona in 1879.
James Stevenson,
Second Annual Report Bureau of Ethnology, 1883, pp. 307-465.

a   Fig. 613, No. 42473, symbolical leaf design.
b   Fig. 615, No. 42471, circular and leaf designs.
c   Fig. 610, No. 42380, oblique bars extending from a center diamond.
d   Fig. 586, No. 42385, undulating bands and triangles in alternate enclosed and upper space.
e   Fig. 592, No. 41298, well formed design with no interest.

The Laguna men are engaged in agriculture and stock raising, while the women, in common with all other Pueblo tribes, are the potters. They produce a variety of exquisite vessels with designs of flowers and bird forms in red and black on a white ground. The pottery is beautifully made, exceptionally well designed, and symmetrically executed.

PLATE 32

a

b

c

d

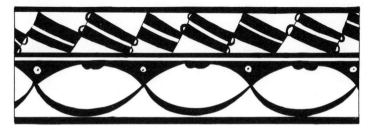

l

Plate 33

COCHITI, NEW MEXICO. PUEBLO GROUP
POTTERY DESIGNS

References:

Illustrated Catalogue of the Collection Obtained from the Indians of New Mexico and Arizona in 1879.
James Stevenson,
Second Annual Report Bureau of Ethnology, 1883, pp. 307-465.
Introduction to American Indian Arts, 1931,
John Sloan and Oliver La Farge
The Rain-makers
Mary R. Coolidge

a Fig. 39733, No. 623, James Stevenson.
b Southwest Museum
c Fig. 39717, No. 631, James Stevenson.
d Fig. 39726, No. 638, James Stevenson.
e Fig. 39718, No. 633, James Stevenson.
f John Sloan and Oliver La Farge.
g Fig. 39733, No. 623, James Stevenson.
h Fig. 39562, No. 640, James Stevenson.
i Fig. 39726, No. 638, James Stevenson.

Cochiti is on the west side of the Rio Grande, twenty-five miles southwest of Santa Fe. Although now of small population, the people of this pueblo claim the ruined towns to the north of their village as the homes of their ancestors. While sharing in the revival of the Pueblo arts and crafts, the ancient symbolism and ceremonies of Cochiti are well preserved.

The pottery designs designate rain, fruition symbols, birds, and flowers, which are arranged with little rhythmic repetition, being scattered over the surface. The pottery, which was formerly black-on-white, now shows some red in the decoration.

PLATE 33

Plate 34

WALPI, ARIZONA. PUEBLO GROUP
POTTERY DESIGNS

Reference:
Illustrated Catalogue of the Collection Obtained from
the Indians of New Mexico and Arizona in 1879.
James Stevenson,
Second Annual Report Bureau of Ethnology, 1883, pp.
307-465.

a   Fig. 514, No. 41609
b   Fig. 531, No. 41391
c   Fig. 518, No. 41363
d   Fig. 518, No. 41363
e   Fig. 532, No. 41390
f   Fig. 519, No. 41366
g   Fig. 514, No. 41609
h   Fig. 514, No. 41609

The pueblo of Walpi is situated on the First Mesa of Hopiland in Arizona, on
one side of which are three rows of terraced houses, and on the other a precipice. A
snake dance, the culmination of a nine-day ceremony for rain, is performed in mid-
summer of every alternate year.

The Hopi of Walpi have developed an exceptionally beautiful type of pottery,
of which there are all too few examples extant. They produced a white decorated ware
similar to that of the Zuñi, using triangular figures, curved line designs and birds.

Commencing about the year 1895, Nampeyo, a woman of the pueblo of Hano, has
practically revolutionized the decoration of Hopi pottery by introducing adaptations
of the designs on prehistoric Hopi earthenware.

PLATE 34

a

b

c

d

e

f

g

h

Plate 35

MODERN HOPI, ARIZONA. PUEBLO GROUP
POTTERY DESIGNS

References:
> Pueblo Pottery Making
> Carl E. Guthe
> The Rain-makers
> Mary R. Coolidge
> The Pueblo Potter
> Ruth Bunzel

a Page 119, No. 14, appendix 2, plate XXXIV, Ruth Bunzel
b Page 118, No. 1, appendix 2, plate XXXIII, Ruth Bunzel
c Page 118, No. 5, appendix 2, plate XXXIII, Ruth Bunzel
d Page 118, No. 2, appendix 2, plate XXXIII, Ruth Bunzel
e Page 119, No. 15, appendix 2, plate XXXIV, Ruth Bunzel

The period of modern Hopi design goes back to about 1850, that is, the period of intimate contact with civilization. The artists are entirely unconscious of the principles of design in their work, and with no guide except perception of form, they produce an accurately finished vessel. A young girl, when given instruction, is told, "Paint anything you like, only put it on straight." The potter is not influenced by the meaning of her design, except in the use of symbols on pottery designed for ceremonial use. Originality and individuality are general with all potters, and she paints to please herself only, although she may be influenced by the prevailing fashion.

PLATE 35

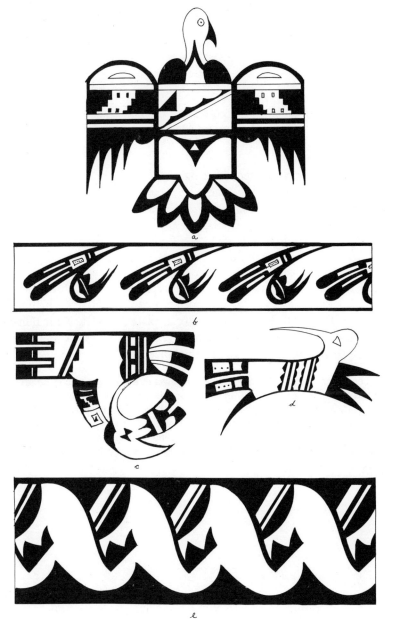

Plate 36

MODERN HOPI, ARIZONA. PUEBLO GROUP
POTTERY DESIGNS

References:
> Pueblo Pottery Making
> Carl E. Guthe
> The Rain-makers
> Mary R. Coolidge
> The Pueblo Potter
> Ruth Bunzel

a   Page 119, No. 17, appendix 2, plate XXXIV, Ruth Bunzel
b   Page 118, No.   3, appendix 2, plate XXXIII, Ruth Bunzel
c   Page 118, No.   1, appendix 2, plate XXXIII, Ruth Bunzel
d   Page 119, No. 18, appendix 2, plate XXXIV, Ruth Bunzel
e   Page 39 b, plate XV, Ruth Bunzel

The present mode of Hopi pottery is a renewal of the ancient type illustrated by Sikyatki ware. In the jars of this modern ware the decoration is principally on the upper part, but extends over the surface to just below the shoulder. The design is bordered at the inner edge by a broad black band, with a similar band at the outer edge. Within a few years this new style has completely displaced the old types of ware, due to a love for the ancient and more pleasing symbolic patterns adapted by Nampeyo, as before mentioned.

PLATE 36

a

b

c

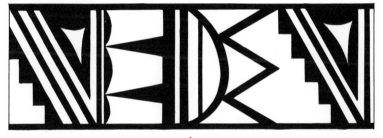

d

e

Plate 37

Zuñi, NEW MEXICO
DANCE MASKS

Reference:
The Zuñi Indians. their Mythology, Esoteric Fraternities, and Ceremonies.
Matilda Coxe Stevenson,
Twenty-third Annual Report Bureau of American Ethnology, 1904, pp. 3-608.

a   Plate LIV, Mask of Sáyatäsha
b   Plate LXXIV, Mask of Hémishikwe
c   Plate LXX, Mask of Úwanami
d   Plate LVa, Mask of Yámuhakto
e   Plate XLIIIb, Mask of Shíwani

The Zuñi have preserved their strong individuality by extreme exclusiveness, and by so doing may claim their high position. They have developed a philosophy which has been profoundly influenced by their environment and upon which is built a highly complicated ceremonial system which has as its object the tribal welfare and success in all undertakings. Their sacred personages, of whom there are very many, are represented in ceremony by performers who wear decorated masks and are elaborately costumed. The masks are usually of leather highly ornamented with symbolic devices.

PLATE 37

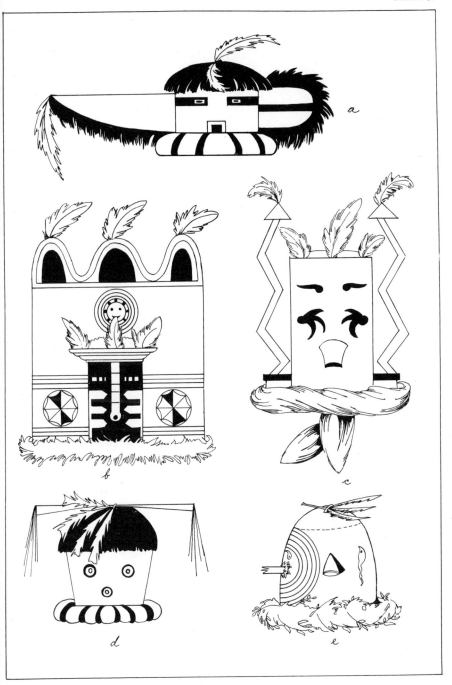

a

b

c

d

e

Plate 38

MARICOPA, ARIZONA
POTTERY, BASKETRY, WEAVING

References:
Yuman Tribes of the Gila River
  Leslie Spier
The North American Indian, vol. II, 1908, pp. 81-88.
Southwest Museum.

a Page 109, plate VIIh, Leslie Spier
b Southwest Museum
c Southwest Museum
d Page 317, fig. 13a, Leslie Spier
e Page 109, Fig. 7c, Leslie Spier
f Page 109, plate VIIf, Leslie Spier
g Page 109, fig. 7e, Leslie Spier

The Maricopa, a small tribe of the Yuman family, reside in southern Arizona not far from Phoenix. They have developed an interesting type of basketry and pottery designs, but borrowed their method of weaving from the Pimas. For their basketry it was customary to use the tisal willow, squaw-weed, root of the tule, and martynia, or devil's claw; leaves of the yucca being used as a filler for the inner coil. The one tool that is always used in basket making is a bone awl, which at death is buried with the artisan.

The designs are striking and varied, the fret being used in combination with circular forms of the swastika. As their artistic faculty developed, practice brought increased skill, and some examples of their baskets, pottery, and weaving are exquisitely beautiful.

PLATE 38

a

b

c

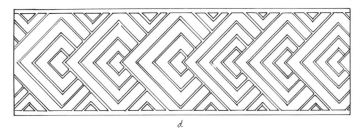

d

e

f

g

Plate 39

References:
  Aboriginal American Basketry: Studies in a Textile Art
    without Machinery.
      Otis Tufton Mason,
  Annual Report of the U. S. National Museum for 1902,
    pp. 171-548.
  Indian Basketry,
    George Wharton James

  a Southwest Museum, pottery design
  b Southwest Museum, beadwork
  c Southwest Museum, beadwork
  d Southwest Museum, beadwork
  e Southwest Museum, beadwork

The Mohave, who gave name to that vast arid waste, the Mohave Desert, are of Yuman stock, like the Maricopas, who have lived for centuries in the valley of the Rio Colorado in California and Arizona. In early times the Mohave were a powerful tribe, but owing to outside influences they have become greatly diminished in number.

The beadwork made by the women is interesting in design; the patterns are made up of so-called symbols combined in various ways. The meaning of these designs is not fixed, so the same symbols are often given different meanings even by persons within the tribe. The Indian artists picture in their work the common objects of everyday life; the great powers of nature, the sun, moon, stars, wind, trees, animals, birds, or whatever might suit their fancy. On clothing, designs were sometimes used that were supposed to have power to protect the wearer from harm. Many of the designs are worked on a white background representing the snow-time, or winter, which was the season when the men went on the war trail to achieve honors and glory. Other colors symbolic of military achievement were red, indicating wounds inflicted or received; yellow the sun-colored war horses, and green, representing the grass or summer. In religious or ceremonial designs, red represents the sunset or thunder; blue, the sky, water or day; yellow, the dawn or sunlight; and black, the night.

PLATE 39

a

b

c

d

e.

Plate 40

SAN CARLOS, ARIZONA AND MESCALERO APACHE, NEW MEXICO BASKET DESIGNS

References:
Basketry of the San Carlos Apache
Helen H. Roberts,
Anthropological Papers of the American Museum of Natural History, 1929, vol. XXXI, pt. 3.
Illustrated History of Baskets and Plates, made by California Indians and many other tribes.
T. A. Roseberry collection

a Page 198, fig. 27, Helen H. Roberts
b Page 198, fig. 27, Helen H. Roberts
c Page 183, fig. 22b, Helen H. Roberts
d Page 178, fig. 19g, Helen H. Roberts
e Plate 18, T. A. Roseberry collection

A small band of people numbering 1172, the San Carlos Apache, live along the main stream and nearer branches of the Gila River to the east of Phoenix, Arizona.

The San Carlos Apache do not use grass in their baskets, but only the shoots of shrubs and young trees, which accounts for the rigidity of their product. Occasionally modern baskets display a touch of red in the color scheme of black and cream, with delightful effect. The material which furnishes the red is the root of the yucca.

These people make three distinct types of baskets: water-jars, carrying baskets, and food bowls of every kind. The bowls are for holding meal, winnowing grain, parching corn, boiling food, mashing berries, mixing dough, and laundry purposes; in fact a bowl or tray is needed by the Indian woman in much the same way as by her white sister. Their twined basketry is crude in texture in design, and in the colors used for the designs. On the other hand, their coiled baskets show the handiwork of an art-loving people. The designs are checkerwork, zigzag, triangles, and diamonds with diagonal, vertical, or horizontal lines. The introduction of human or animal figures, sometimes grotesque, is of comparatively recent origin. The square and rectangle are entirely absent as separate figures, occuring only in some sort of checker formation. Triangles and diamonds are worked in solid colors, usually black, since the background is cream. The adaptation of the size of design to the form of the background field illustrates clearly that the San Carlos artistic sense is of an unusually high order.

PLATE 40

Plate 41

WHITE MOUNTAIN, ARIZONA AND MESCALERO APACHE, NEW MEXICO
BASKET AND DRESS ORNAMENT

References:
A Study of the Textile Art in its Relation to the Development of Form and Color.
William H. Holmes,
Sixth Annual Report Bureau of Ethnology, 1888, pp. 189-252.
Annual Report of the Smithsonian Institution, 1928.
Specimens from Southwest Museum.
Indian Basketry,
George Wharton James

a   Southwest Museum
b   Southwest Museum
c   Plate 17, Report Smithsonian Institution, 1928
d   Page 223, fig. 325, William H. Holmes
e   Southwest Museum
f   Southwest Museum

The Apache are to be found in New Mexico and Arizona. A warlike nomadic people, the terror of the early white settlers of the Southwest, yet when intelligently treated, no more appreciative or tractable Indians are to be found.

The Apache are expert basket-makers, proud of the fineness of their work, extremely poetic in the designs they conceive, and artistic in their arrangement. The designs usually consist of small figures with a sense of ease approaching realism.

PLATE 41

Plate 42

PAPAGO, ARIZONA-SONORA
POTTERY DESIGNS

References:
Basketry of the Papago and Pima,
Mary L. Kissell,
Anthropological Papers of the American Museum of
Natural History, 1916, vol. XVII, pp. 115-264.

a   Page 213, fig. 59e
b   Page 213, fig. 59f
c   Page 218, fig. 64b
d   Page 219, fig. 65c
e   Page 239, fig. 77
f   Page 240, fig. 78

The Papago live in southern Arizona and northwestern Sonora. Possibly in no other spot in North America has the Indian been less influenced by white men, so that old customs persist, even to the tattooing of the face by older men and women.

Like all desert regions, plant growth was hindered in its struggle for existence, and the desert vegetation exerted an influence upon the activities of the tribes, and the tribes in turn have adapted themselves to the limitations of the desert, hence much effort and skill were required to discover the materials most suitable for basket-making. Excellent coiled baskets have been produced by Papago women, but it is said that many of them have been sacrificed by burning on the death of the owners.

PLATE 42

a

b

c

d

e

f

Plate 43

References:

Basketry of the Papago and Pima,
Mary L. Kissell,
Anthropological Papers of the American Museum of
Natural History, 1916, vol. XVII, pp. 115-264.

a   Page 221, fig. 67d
b   Page 223, fig. 69
c   Page 221, fig. 67c
d   Page 213, fig. 59b
e   Page 239, fig. 77
f   Page 216, fig. 62c

Distinctive differences between the basketry designs of the Pima and the Papago are found. The influence of the environment is felt, since the supply of martynia gives Papago a dominance of dark over light in their baskets. Aside from the dissimilarity in dark and light, the bands differ obviously in shape, proportion, and general contour. One is impressed by the strong feeling for large masses of dark and light in comparison to the feeling for line of the Pima. The Papago woman deals mostly with a horizontal line in her work, which gives a restful quality to the design. They have a distinct number of typical designs, namely, the encircling fret, the horizontal band arranged in a variety of ways, and the vertical fret.

Papago design is dignified and reserved, handled in a simple, strong, and direct manner.

PLATE 43

a

b

c

d

e

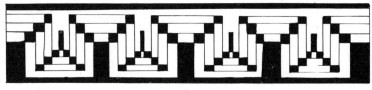

f

Plate 44

Reference:
The Pima Indians
Frank Russell,
Twenty-sixth Annual Report Bureau of American Eth-

nology, 1908, pp. 3-389.
a   Plate XXVII, d
b   Plate XXVIII, a
c   Plate XXV, a
d   Plate XXVII, e
e   Plate XVIII, c
f   Plate XIX, f

The Pima inhabit a reservation in southern Arizona not far from Phoenix, and have always been noted for their quiet and peaceful character. They have developed a high type of basketry which contains some intricate patterns that resemble Greek and Oriental figures; in the variations of the swastika alone they show splendid examples. Many of their designs represent the source of water supply in the center, with radiating geometric lines representing the winding streams.

In the construction of their baskets the Pima use the tisal willow, squaw weed, skunk weed, the root of the tule, and martyina, or devil's claw.

PLATE 44

Plate 45

PIMA, ARIZONA
BASKETRY DESIGNS

Reference:
> The Pima Indians
> Frank Russell,
> Twenty-sixth Annual Report Bureau of American Eth-
> nology, 1908, pp 3, 390.

> a   Plate XXXII, c
> b   Plate XXX, h
> c   Plate XXIX, c
> d   Plate XX, e
> e   Plate XXXI, f
> f   Page 130, fig. 55

In Pima basketry there is a dominance of light over dark color, with a feeling for line which is expressed in a network of black. Horizontal lines are used in a secondary way, being held in subservience to a more dominant motif, the spiral and whorl. The patterns are the fret, rectangular whorl, triangular whorl, spiral rosette, and terrace. The fret is the oldest and most common design. The whorl consists of four central twirling rectangular arms with a repeating whorl at the rim. Obliques are frequently composed of a line of small triangles forming a terraced design.

Pima work is replete with action and grace; it is elaborate, delicate, and intricate; the technique is clear-cut and perfect in craftsmanship.

PLATE 45

a

b

c

d

e

f

Plate 46

References:
Aboriginal American Basketry: Studies in a Textile Art without Machinery.
Otis Tufton Mason,
Annual Report of the U. S. National Museum for 1902, pp. 171-548.
Basketry of the San Carlos Apache
Helen H. Roberts,
Anthropological Papers of the American Museum of Natural History, 1929, vol. XXXI, pt. 3.

a Plate 231, vol. 2, Otis Tufton Mason
b Plate 231, vol. 2, Otis Tufton Mason
c Page 180, fig. 21, Helen H. Roberts
d Page 179, fig. 20, Helen H. Roberts
e Plate 231, Otis Tufton Mason
f Plate 231, Otis Tufton Mason

The Chemehuevi live along the Colorado river north of the Mohave. They produce basketry similar to that of the San Carlos Apache, hence there is a tendency to confuse the two.

Horizontal arrangements are typical, while radiating or whorling distributions are rare. This difference in design arrangement is one of the distinguishing features of the basketry of the Chemehuevi and Apache, also the finish of the rim coil; were it not for this it would be difficult to discriminate the products of the two tribes. Hence it is more by feel, which comes only with study, than by rule that the basket lover may learn to recognize the work of the various Indians.

PLATE 46

Plate 47

NAVAHO, ARIZONA-NEW MEXICO. NOMADIC GROUP
MODERN RUG DESIGNS

References:
The Navaho and his Blanket
U. S. Hollister
Navaho Weaving
Charles Avery Amsden
Design detail from blankets, Southwest Museum
Design detail from blankets, Mrs. Kenneth Worthen
Design detail from blankets, Mrs. F. R. Smith

a Mrs. Kenneth Worthen
b Southwest Museum
c Mrs. Kenneth Worthen
d Southwest Museum
e Southwest Museum
f Mrs. F. R. Smith
g Mrs. F. R. Smith
h Mrs. Kenneth Worthen
i Southwest Museum
j Mrs. F. R. Smith

The Navaho are a semi-nomadic Athapascan tribe occupying a reservation in northern Arizona, northwest New Mexico, and southern Utah. Numbering about 40,000, they are the most populous tribe in the United States.

They are a picturesque people whose principal interests are blanket weaving, sheep herding, and the manufacture of silver and turquoise jewelry. The Navaho shear their sheep, wash, dye, card, spin, and weave the wool into attractive and valuable blankets. The primitive art of weaving is many centuries old, but so far as known the Navaho acquired the art from captive Pueblo women not earlier than the latter part of the eighteenth century.

PLATE 47

Plate 48

NAVAHO, ARIZONA-NEW MEXICO. NOMADIC GROUP
PATTERNS AND FIGURES FROM DRY PAINTINGS OF DŚILYIDJE-QÁCAL.

Reference:
> The Mountain Chant.
> Washington Matthews,
> Fifth Annual Report Bureau of Ethnology, 1887, pp.
> 379-467.

a   Plate XVI
b   Plate XVI
c   Plate XV
d   Plate XV
e   Plate XVI
f   Plate XVI

Sand to the depth of two inches is spread on the floor, then smoothed and evened with a curved stick; on this sand the artist works from the center outward with colors made by a man sitting at the east. Yellow, red, and white are made by grinding native rocks; black is made from charcoal. Black and white are mixed to produce a gray-blue.

The four sacred colors of the cardinal points are, white for the East, blue for the West, yellow for the South, and black for the North.

The artist then takes a pinch of the desired color between his thumb and forefinger and lets it trickle in the line of his proposed design, when the pattern is finished, with its exquisite color and detail, a rare work of art is produced.

PLATE 48

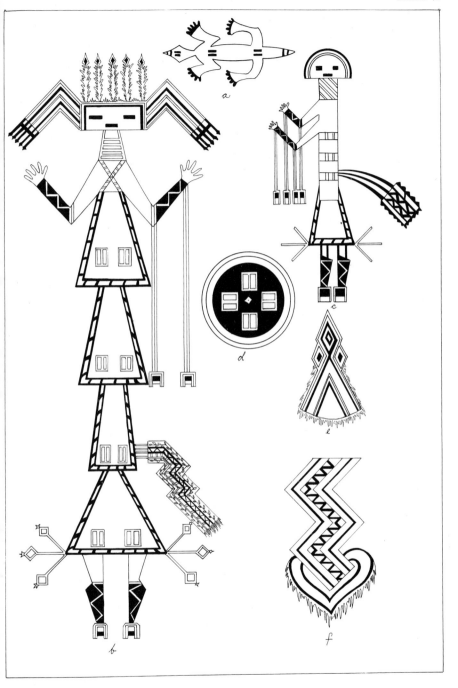

Plate 49

NAVAHO, ARIZONA-NEW MEXICO. NOMADIC GROUP
PATTERNS AND FIGURES FROM DRY PAINTINGS OF DSILYIDJE-QÁCAL.

Reference:
The Mountain Chant.
Fifth Annual Report Bureau of Ethnology, 1887, pp. 379-467.

a   Plate XVII
b   Plate XVII
c   Plate XVII
d   Plate XVII
e   Plate XVII
f   Plate XVII
g   Plate XVII
h   Plate XVII
i   Plate XVIII

Every ceremony has its own dry painting, and these represent a very old traditional art which was borrowed from the Pueblos. The essence of Navaho art is an arrangement and repetition of a few elements, either in stripes or around a central motif, or spotting against a plain or striped background. The keynote of their work is a large mass of perfect simplicity, and continuous repetition of quiet inert design.

PLATE 49

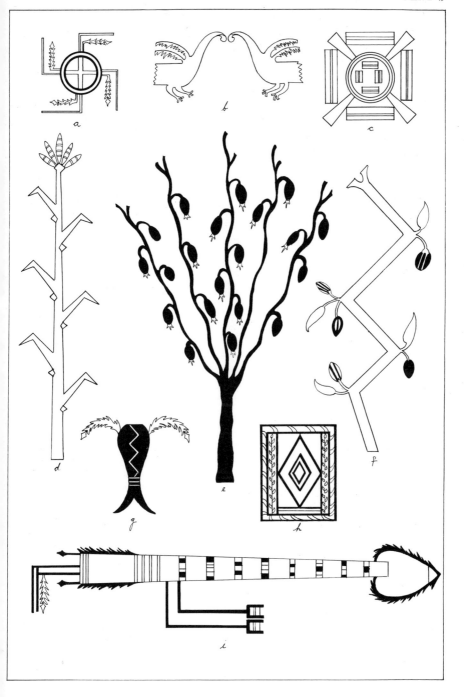

Plate 50

NAVAHO, ARIZONA-NEW MEXICO. NOMADIC GROUP
ANCIENT AND MODERN RUG DESIGNS

References:
Navaho Weavers and their Work.
Washington Matthews,
Third Annual Report Bureau of Ethnology, 1884, pp. 371-391.
Design detail from blankets, Southwest Museum.
Design detail from blanket, collection of Mrs. Kenneth Worthen.

a   Southwest Museum
b   Southwest Museum
c   Southwest Museum
d   Mrs. Kenneth Worthen
e   Southwest Museum
f   Southwest Museum

The women who have controlled the weaving industry for two centuries originally had only three natural colors to use, a rusty black, white, and a brownish gray; herbs and a desert brush were used to produce livlier shades. To intensify the black a dye was made of sumac, ochre, and piñon boiled together. Similarly was invented a dark blue, several shades of yellow, and a reddish color.

The women who for generations have been weaving from their imagination follow no visible pattern, yet the design, color, and proportion in the hands of an experienced weaver come out nearly perfect.

PLATE 50

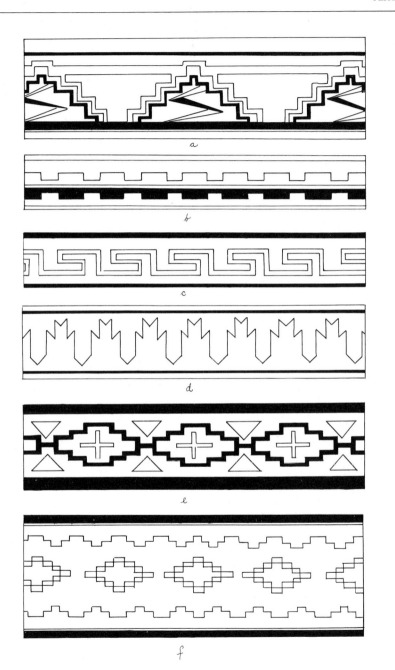

a

b

c

d

e

f

A CATALOGUE OF SELECTED DOVER BOOKS
IN ALL FIELDS OF INTEREST

A CATALOGUE OF SELECTED DOVER BOOKS
IN ALL FIELDS OF INTEREST

LEATHER TOOLING AND CARVING, Chris H. Groneman. One of few books concentrating on tooling and carving, with complete instructions and grid designs for 39 projects ranging from bookmarks to bags. 148 illustrations. 111pp. 7⁷⁄₈ x 10.
23061-9 Pa. $2.50

THE CODEX NUTTALL, A PICTURE MANUSCRIPT FROM ANCIENT MEXICO, as first edited by Zelia Nuttall. Only inexpensive edition, in full color, of a pre-Columbian Mexican (Mixtec) book. 88 color plates show kings, gods, heroes, temples, sacrifices. New explanatory, historical introduction by Arthur G. Miller. 96pp. 11³⁄₈ x 8½.
23168-2 Pa. $7.50

AMERICAN PRIMITIVE PAINTING, Jean Lipman. Classic collection of an enduring American tradition. 109 plates, 8 in full color—portraits, landscapes, Biblical and historical scenes, etc., showing family groups, farm life, and so on. 80pp. of lucid text. 8³⁄₈ x 11¼.
22815-0 Pa. $4.00

WILL BRADLEY: HIS GRAPHIC ART, edited by Clarence P. Hornung. Striking collection of work by foremost practitioner of Art Nouveau in America: posters, cover designs, sample pages, advertisements, other illustrations. 97 plates, including 8 in full color and 19 in two colors. 97pp. 9³⁄₈ x 12¼.
20701-3 Pa. $4.00
22120-2 Clothbd. $10.00

THE UNDERGROUND SKETCHBOOK OF JAN FAUST, Jan Faust. 101 bitter, horrifying, black-humorous, penetrating sketches on sex, war, greed, various liberations, etc. Sometimes sexual, but not pornographic. Not for prudish. 101pp. 6½ x 9¼.
22740-5 Pa. $1.50

THE GIBSON GIRL AND HER AMERICA, Charles Dana Gibson. 155 finest drawings of effervescent world of 1900-1910: the Gibson Girl and her loves, amusements, adventures, Mr. Pipp, etc. Selected by E. Gillon; introduction by Henry Pitz. 144pp. 8¼ x 11³⁄₈.
21986-0 Pa. $3.50

STAINED GLASS CRAFT, J.A.F. Divine, G. Blachford. One of the very few books that tell the beginner exactly what he needs to know: planning cuts, making shapes, avoiding design weaknesses, fitting glass, etc. 93 illustrations. 115pp.
22812-6 Pa. $1.50

CATALOGUE OF DOVER BOOKS

THE FITZWILLIAM VIRGINAL BOOK, edited by J. Fuller Maitland, W.B. Squire. Famous early 17th century collection of keyboard music, 300 works by Morley, Byrd, Bull, Gibbons, etc. Modern notation. Total of 938pp. 8⅜ x 11.
ECE 21068-5, 21069-3 Pa., Two vol. set $12.00

COMPLETE STRING QUARTETS, Wolfgang A. Mozart. Breitkopf and Härtel edition. All 23 string quartets plus alternate slow movement to K156. Study score. 277pp. 9⅜ x 12¼. 22372-8 Pa. $6.00

COMPLETE SONG CYCLES, Franz Schubert. Complete piano, vocal music of Die Schöne Müllerin, Die Winterreise, Schwanengesang. Also Drinker English singing translations. Breitkopf and Härtel edition. 217pp. 9⅜ x 12¼.
22649-2 Pa. $4.00

THE COMPLETE PRELUDES AND ETUDES FOR PIANOFORTE SOLO, Alexander Scriabin. All the preludes and etudes including many perfectly spun miniatures. Edited by K.N. Igumnov and Y.I. Mil'shteyn. 250pp. 9 x 12. 22919-X Pa. $5.00

TRISTAN UND ISOLDE, Richard Wagner. Full orchestral score with complete instrumentation. Do not confuse with piano reduction. Commentary by Felix Mottl, great Wagnerian conductor and scholar. Study score. 655pp. 8⅛ x 11.
22915-7 Pa. $10.00

FAVORITE SONGS OF THE NINETIES, ed. Robert Fremont. Full reproduction, including covers, of 88 favorites: Ta-Ra-Ra-Boom-De-Aye, The Band Played On, Bird in a Gilded Cage, Under the Bamboo Tree, After the Ball, etc. 401pp. 9 x 12.
EBE 21536-9 Pa. $6.95

SOUSA'S GREAT MARCHES IN PIANO TRANSCRIPTION: ORIGINAL SHEET MUSIC OF 23 WORKS, John Philip Sousa. Selected by Lester S. Levy. Playing edition includes: The Stars and Stripes Forever, The Thunderer, The Gladiator, King Cotton, Washington Post, much more. 24 illustrations. 111pp. 9 x 12.
USO 23132-1 Pa. $3.50

CLASSIC PIANO RAGS, selected with an introduction by Rudi Blesh. Best ragtime music (1897-1922) by Scott Joplin, James Scott, Joseph F. Lamb, Tom Turpin, 9 others. Printed from best original sheet music, plus covers. 364pp. 9 x 12.
EBE 20469-3 Pa. $6.95

ANALYSIS OF CHINESE CHARACTERS, C.D. Wilder, J.H. Ingram. 1000 most important characters analyzed according to primitives, phonetics, historical development. Traditional method offers mnemonic aid to beginner, intermediate student of Chinese, Japanese. 365pp. 23045-7 Pa. $4.00

MODERN CHINESE: A BASIC COURSE, Faculty of Peking University. Self study, classroom course in modern Mandarin. Records contain phonetics, vocabulary, sentences, lessons. 249 page book contains all recorded text, translations, grammar, vocabulary, exercises. Best course on market. 3 12" 33⅓ monaural records, book, album. 98832-5 Set $12.50

CATALOGUE OF DOVER BOOKS

THE JOURNAL OF HENRY D. THOREAU, edited by Bradford Torrey, F.H. Allen. Complete reprinting of 14 volumes, 1837-1861, over two million words; the sourcebooks for Walden, etc. Definitive. All original sketches, plus 75 photographs. Introduction by Walter Harding. Total of 1804pp. 8½ x 12¼.
20312-3, 20313-1 Clothbd., Two vol. set $50.00

MASTERS OF THE DRAMA, John Gassner. Most comprehensive history of the drama, every tradition from Greeks to modern Europe and America, including Orient. Covers 800 dramatists, 2000 plays; biography, plot summaries, criticism, theatre history, etc. 77 illustrations. 890pp. 20100-7 Clothbd. $10.00

GHOST AND HORROR STORIES OF AMBROSE BIERCE, Ambrose Bierce. 23 modern horror stories: The Eyes of the Panther, The Damned Thing, etc., plus the dream-essay Visions of the Night. Edited by E.F. Bleiler. 199pp. 20767-6 Pa. $2.00

BEST GHOST STORIES, Algernon Blackwood. 13 great stories by foremost British 20th century supernaturalist. The Willows, The Wendigo, Ancient Sorceries, others. Edited by E.F. Bleiler. 366pp. USO 22977-7 Pa. $3.00

THE BEST TALES OF HOFFMANN, E.T.A. Hoffmann. 10 of Hoffmann's most important stories, in modern re-editings of standard translations: Nutcracker and the King of Mice, The Golden Flowerpot, etc. 7 illustrations by Hoffmann. Edited by E.F. Bleiler. 458pp. 21793-0 Pa. $3.95

BEST GHOST STORIES OF J.S. LEFANU, J. Sheridan LeFanu. 16 stories by greatest Victorian master: Green Tea, Carmilla, Haunted Baronet, The Familiar, etc. Mostly unavailable elsewhere. Edited by E.F. Bleiler. 8 illustrations. 467pp.
20415-4 Pa. $4.00

SUPERNATURAL HORROR IN LITERATURE, H.P. Lovecraft. Great modern American supernaturalist brilliantly surveys history of genre to 1930's, summarizing, evaluating scores of books. Necessary for every student, lover of form. Introduction by E.F. Bleiler. 111pp. 20105-8 Pa. $1.50

THREE GOTHIC NOVELS, ed. by E.F. Bleiler. Full texts Castle of Otranto, Walpole; Vathek, Beckford; The Vampyre, Polidori; Fragment of a Novel, Lord Byron. 331pp. 21232-7 Pa. $3.00

SEVEN SCIENCE FICTION NOVELS, H.G. Wells. Full novels. First Men in the Moon, Island of Dr. Moreau, War of the Worlds, Food of the Gods, Invisible Man, Time Machine, In the Days of the Comet. A basic science-fiction library. 1015pp.
USO 20264-X Clothbd. $6.00

LADY AUDLEY'S SECRET, Mary E. Braddon. Great Victorian mystery classic, beautifully plotted, suspenseful; praised by Thackeray, Boucher, Starrett, others. What happened to beautiful, vicious Lady Audley's husband? Introduction by Norman Donaldson. 286pp. 23011-2 Pa. $3.00

CATALOGUE OF DOVER BOOKS

DRIED FLOWERS, Sarah Whitlock and Martha Rankin. Concise, clear, practical guide to dehydration, glycerinizing, pressing plant material, and more. Covers use of silica gel. 12 drawings. Originally titled "New Techniques with Dried Flowers." 32pp. 21802-3 Pa. $1.00

ABC OF POULTRY RAISING, J.H. Florea. Poultry expert, editor tells how to raise chickens on home or small business basis. Breeds, feeding, housing, laying, etc. Very concrete, practical. 50 illustrations. 256pp. 23201-8 Pa. $3.00

HOW INDIANS USE WILD PLANTS FOR FOOD, MEDICINE & CRAFTS, Frances Densmore. Smithsonian, Bureau of American Ethnology report presents wealth of material on nearly 200 plants used by Chippewas of Minnesota and Wisconsin. 33 plates plus 122pp. of text. 6⅛ x 9¼. 23019-8 Pa. $2.50

THE HERBAL OR GENERAL HISTORY OF PLANTS, John Gerard. The 1633 edition revised and enlarged by Thomas Johnson. Containing almost 2850 plant descriptions and 2705 superb illustrations, Gerard's Herbal is a monumental work, the book all modern English herbals are derived from, and the one herbal every serious enthusiast should have in its entirety. Original editions are worth perhaps $750. 1678pp. 8½ x 12¼. 23147-X Clothbd. $50.00

A MODERN HERBAL, Margaret Grieve. Much the fullest, most exact, most useful compilation of herbal material. Gigantic alphabetical encyclopedia, from aconite to zedoary, gives botanical information, medical properties, folklore, economic uses, and much else. Indispensable to serious reader. 161 illustrations. 888pp. 6½ x 9¼. USO 22798-7, 22799-5 Pa., Two vol. set $10.00

HOW TO KNOW THE FERNS, Frances T. Parsons. Delightful classic. Identification, fern lore, for Eastern and Central U.S.A. Has introduced thousands to interesting life form. 99 illustrations. 215pp. 20740-4 Pa. $2.50

THE MUSHROOM HANDBOOK, Louis C.C. Krieger. Still the best popular handbook. Full descriptions of 259 species, extremely thorough text, habitats, luminescence, poisons, folklore, etc. 32 color plates; 126 other illustrations. 560pp. 21861-9 Pa. $4.50

HOW TO KNOW THE WILD FRUITS, Maude G. Peterson. Classic guide covers nearly 200 trees, shrubs, smaller plants of the U.S. arranged by color of fruit and then by family. Full text provides names, descriptions, edibility, uses. 80 illustrations. 400pp. 22943-2 Pa. $3.00

COMMON WEEDS OF THE UNITED STATES, U.S. Department of Agriculture. Covers 220 important weeds with illustration, maps, botanical information, plant lore for each. Over 225 illustrations. 463pp. 6⅛ x 9¼. 20504-5 Pa. $4.50

HOW TO KNOW THE WILD FLOWERS, Mrs. William S. Dana. Still best popular book for East and Central USA. Over 500 plants easily identified, with plant lore; arranged according to color and flowering time. 174 plates. 459pp. 20332-8 Pa. $3.50

CATALOGUE OF DOVER BOOKS

150 MASTERPIECES OF DRAWING, edited by Anthony Toney. 150 plates, early 15th century to end of 18th century; Rembrandt, Michelangelo, Dürer, Fragonard, Watteau, Wouwerman, many others. 150pp. 8⅜ x 11¼. 21032-4 Pa. $3.50

THE GOLDEN AGE OF THE POSTER, Hayward and Blanche Cirker. 70 extraordinary posters in full colors, from Maîtres de l'Affiche, Mucha, Lautrec, Bradley, Cheret, Beardsley, many others. 9⅜ x 12¼. 22753-7 Pa. $4.95
21718-3 Clothbd. $7.95

SIMPLICISSIMUS, selection, translations and text by Stanley Appelbaum. 180 satirical drawings, 16 in full color, from the famous German weekly magazine in the years 1896 to 1926. 24 artists included: Grosz, Kley, Pascin, Kubin, Kollwitz, plus Heine, Thöny, Bruno Paul, others. 172pp. 8½ x 12¼. 23098-8 Pa. $5.00
23099-6 Clothbd. $10.00

THE EARLY WORK OF AUBREY BEARDSLEY, Aubrey Beardsley. 157 plates, 2 in color: Manon Lescaut, Madame Bovary, Morte d'Arthur, Salome, other. Introduction by H. Marillier. 175pp. 8½ x 11. 21816-3 Pa. $3.50

THE LATER WORK OF AUBREY BEARDSLEY, Aubrey Beardsley. Exotic masterpieces of full maturity: Venus and Tannhäuser, Lysistrata, Rape of the Lock, Volpone, Savoy material, etc. 174 plates, 2 in color. 176pp. 8½ x 11. 21817-1 Pa. $3.75

DRAWINGS OF WILLIAM BLAKE, William Blake. 92 plates from Book of Job, Divine Comedy, Paradise Lost, visionary heads, mythological figures, Laocoön, etc. Selection, introduction, commentary by Sir Geoffrey Keynes. 178pp. 8½ x 11. 22303-5 Pa. $3.50

LONDON: A PILGRIMAGE, Gustave Doré, Blanchard Jerrold. Squalor, riches, misery, beauty of mid-Victorian metropolis; 55 wonderful plates, 125 other illustrations, full social, cultural text by Jerrold. 191pp. of text. 8⅛ x 11. 22306-X Pa. $5.00

THE COMPLETE WOODCUTS OF ALBRECHT DÜRER, edited by Dr. W. Kurth. 346 in all: Old Testament, St. Jerome, Passion, Life of Virgin, Apocalypse, many others. Introduction by Campbell Dodgson. 285pp. 8½ x 12¼. 21097-9 Pa. $6.00

THE DISASTERS OF WAR, Francisco Goya. 83 etchings record horrors of Napoleonic wars in Spain and war in general. Reprint of 1st edition, plus 3 additional plates. Introduction by Philip Hofer. 97pp. 9⅜ x 8¼. 21872-4 Pa. $2.50

ENGRAVINGS OF HOGARTH, William Hogarth. 101 of Hogarth's greatest works: Rake's Progress, Harlot's Progress, Illustrations for Hudibras, Midnight Modern Conversation, Before and After, Beer Street and Gin Lane, many more. Full commentary. 256pp. 11 x 14. 22479-1 Pa. $6.00
23023-6 Clothbd. $13.50

PRIMITIVE ART, Franz Boas. Great anthropologist on ceramics, textiles, wood, stone, metal, etc.; patterns, technology, symbols, styles. All areas, but fullest on Northwest Coast Indians. 350 illustrations. 378pp. 20025-6 Pa. $3.50

JEWISH GREETING CARDS, Ed Sibbett, Jr. 16 cards to cut and color. Three say "Happy Chanukah," one "Happy New Year," others have no message, show stars of David, Torahs, wine cups, other traditional themes. 16 envelopes. 8¼ x 11.
23225-5 Pa. $2.00

AUBREY BEARDSLEY GREETING CARD BOOK, Aubrey Beardsley. Edited by Theodore Menten. 16 elegant yet inexpensive greeting cards let you combine your own sentiments with subtle Art Nouveau lines. 16 different Aubrey Beardsley designs that you can color or not, as you wish. 16 envelopes. 64pp. 8¼ x 11.
23173-9 Pa. $2.00

RECREATIONS IN THE THEORY OF NUMBERS, Albert Beiler. Number theory, an inexhaustible source of puzzles, recreations, for beginners and advanced. Divisors, perfect numbers. scales of notation, etc. 349pp.
21096-0 Pa. $2.50

AMUSEMENTS IN MATHEMATICS, Henry E. Dudeney. One of largest puzzle collections, based on algebra, arithmetic, permutations, probability, plane figure dissection, properties of numbers, by one of world's foremost puzzlists. Solutions. 450 illustrations. 258pp.
20473-1 Pa. $2.75

MATHEMATICS, MAGIC AND MYSTERY, Martin Gardner. Puzzle editor for Scientific American explains math behind: card tricks, stage mind reading, coin and match tricks, counting out games, geometric dissections. Probability, sets, theory of numbers, clearly explained. Plus more than 400 tricks, guaranteed to work. 135 illustrations. 176pp.
20335-2 Pa. $2.00

BEST MATHEMATICAL PUZZLES OF SAM LOYD, edited by Martin Gardner. Bizarre, original, whimsical puzzles by America's greatest puzzler. From fabulously rare Cyclopedia, including famous 14-15 puzzles, the Horse of a Different Color, 115 more. Elementary math. 150 illustrations. 167pp.
20498-7 Pa. $2.00

MATHEMATICAL PUZZLES FOR BEGINNERS AND ENTHUSIASTS, Geoffrey Mott-Smith. 189 puzzles from easy to difficult involving arithmetic, logic, algebra, properties of digits, probability. Explanation of math behind puzzles. 135 illustrations. 248pp.
20198-8 Pa. $2.00

BIG BOOK OF MAZES AND LABYRINTHS, Walter Shepherd. Classical, solid, and ripple mazes; short path and avoidance labyrinths; more — 50 mazes and labyrinths in all. 12 other figures. Full solutions. 112pp. 8⅛ x 11.
22951-3 Pa. $2.00

COIN GAMES AND PUZZLES, Maxey Brooke. 60 puzzles, games and stunts — from Japan, Korea, Africa and the ancient world, by Dudeney and the other great puzzlers, as well as Maxey Brooke's own creations. Full solutions. 67 illustrations. 94pp.
22893-2 Pa. $1.25

HAND SHADOWS TO BE THROWN UPON THE WALL, Henry Bursill. Wonderful Victorian novelty tells how to make flying birds, dog, goose, deer, and 14 others. 32pp. 6½ x 9¼.
21779-5 Pa. $1.00

BUILD YOUR OWN LOW-COST HOME, L.O. Anderson, H.F. Zornig. U.S. Dept. of Agriculture sets of plans, full, detailed, for 11 houses: A-Frame, circular, conventional. Also construction manual. Save hundreds of dollars. 204pp. 11 x 16.
21525-3 Pa. $5.95

HOW TO BUILD A WOOD-FRAME HOUSE, L.O. Anderson. Comprehensive, easy to follow U.S. Government manual: placement, foundations, framing, sheathing, roof, insulation, plaster, finishing — almost everything else. 179 illustrations. 223pp. 7⅞ x 10¾.
22954-8 Pa. $3.50

CONCRETE, MASONRY AND BRICKWORK, U.S. Department of the Army. Practical handbook for the home owner and small builder, manual contains basic principles, techniques, and important background information on construction with concrete, concrete blocks, and brick. 177 figures, 37 tables. 200pp. 6½ x 9¼.
23203-4 Pa: $4.00

THE STANDARD BOOK OF QUILT MAKING AND COLLECTING, Marguerite Ickis. Full information, full-sized patterns for making 46 traditional quilts, also 150 other patterns. Quilted cloths, lamé, satin quilts, etc. 483 illustrations. 273pp. 6⅞ x 9⅝.
20582-7 Pa. $3.50

101 PATCHWORK PATTERNS, Ruby S. McKim. 101 beautiful, immediately useable patterns, full-size, modern and traditional. Also general information, estimating, quilt lore. 124pp. 7⅞ x 10¾.
20773-0 Pa. $2.50

KNIT YOUR OWN NORWEGIAN SWEATERS, Dale Yarn Company. Complete instructions for 50 authentic sweaters, hats, mittens, gloves, caps, etc. Thoroughly modern designs that command high prices in stores. 24 patterns, 24 color photographs. Nearly 100 charts and other illustrations. 58pp. 8⅜ x 11¼.
23031-7 Pa. $2.50

IRON-ON TRANSFER PATTERNS FOR CREWEL AND EMBROIDERY FROM EARLY AMERICAN SOURCES, edited by Rita Weiss. 75 designs, borders, alphabets, from traditional American sources printed on translucent paper in transfer ink. Reuseable. Instructions. Test patterns. 24pp. 8¼ x 11.
23162-3 Pa. $1.50

AMERICAN INDIAN NEEDLEPOINT DESIGNS FOR PILLOWS, BELTS, HANDBAGS AND OTHER PROJECTS, Roslyn Epstein. 37 authentic American Indian designs adapted for modern needlepoint projects. Grid backing makes designs easily transferable to canvas. 48pp. 8¼ x 11.
22973-4 Pa. $1.50

CHARTED FOLK DESIGNS FOR CROSS-STITCH EMBROIDERY, Maria Foris & Andreas Foris. 278 charted folk designs, most in 2 colors, from Danube region: florals, fantastic beasts, geometrics, traditional symbols, more. Border and central patterns. 77pp. 8¼ x 11.
USO 23191-7 Pa. $2.00

Prices subject to change without notice.
Available at your book dealer or write for free catalogue to Dept. GI, Dover Publications, Inc., 180 Varick St., N.Y., N.Y. 10014. Dover publishes more than 150 books each year on science, elementary and advanced mathematics, biology, music, art, literary history, social sciences and other areas.